Magical Forest mazes

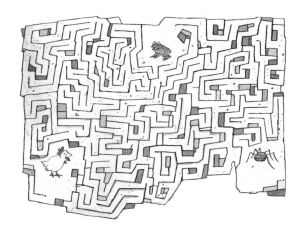

Magical Forest mazes

maze craze

Don-Oliver Matthies

Sterling Publishing Co., Inc.
New York

Library of Congress Cataloging-in-Publication Data Available

10   9   8   7   6

Published in 2004 by Sterling Publishing Co., Inc.
387 Park Avenue South, New York, NY 10016
Originally published in Germany in 2004 under the title
Zauberei im Hexenwald by Edition Bücherbär im Arena
Verlag GmbH, Rottendorfer Str. 16, D-97074 Würzburg
Copyright © 2004 by Edition Bücherbär im Arena Verlag GmbH
English translation by Daniel M. Shea and Nicole Franke
English translation © 2004 by Sterling Publishing Co., Inc.
Distributed in Canada by Sterling Publishing
C/o Canadian Manda Group, 165 Dufferin Street
Toronto, Ontario, Canada M6K 3H6
Distributed in the United Kingdom by GMC Distribution Services,
Castle Place, 166 High Street, Lewes, East Sussex, England BN7 1XU
Distributed in Australia by Capricorn Link (Australia) Pty Ltd.
P.O. Box 704, Windsor, NSW 2756, Australia

Sterling ISBN-13: 978-1-4027-1758-1
        ISBN-10: 1-4027-1758-X

For information about custom editions, special sales, premium and
corporate purchases, please contact Sterling Special Sales
Department at 800-805-5489 or specialsales@sterlingpub.com

Draw a picture or place a
photograph of yourself here:

This book belongs to:

_____

Meet Griselda and her pet frog Rudy. They
live in the Magical Forest.

This is Griselda and Rudy's house. Can you find your way through it?

start

end

During her morning walk, Griselda decides she is going to make a mushroom omelet for breakfast. There's only one problem: one mushroom is poisonous and the other is not. Which way leads to the nonpoisonous mushroom?

While she eats, Griselda's magic potion begins to burn and smoke fills up her entire kitchen!

What a mess she has on her hands now! Griselda decides to use a spell to clean up the kitchen. Uh-oh! She says the wrong words and poor Rudy gets caught in the middle of the spell. Solve the maze to see what Rudy will turn into.

start

chicken

spider

Griselda's magic tricks do not seem to be working today! Griselda now has to do the dishes by hand—the old fashioned way.

Even a simple magic spell to light the fire doesn't work! A spark flies onto her favorite dress and makes a huge hole in it.

end

start

Griselda gives up on her magic spells and decides to practice flying her broom. From which point did Griselda start? Afterwards, try solving the maze to get to the top of the tower.

Later in the afternoon, Griselda receives an invitation to the Witch Dance tomorrow night at midnight. Which animal brought her the invitation?

Seagull

Owl

Bat

Griselda suddenly begins to panic. "Rudy is a chicken; I burned a hole in my favorite dress; and none of my spells are working," she thinks to herself. "I cannot let the witches see me in such a mess!" Griselda needs some help. Move only through the stars to find out who can help her.

On her way to the Old Witch, Griselda runs into her friend Gary the Gnome. He hasn't seen the Old Witch but tells Griselda to ask Uma the Unicorn.

start

end

Uma tells Griselda that the Old Witch lives deep in the Magical Forest. She will have to travel through the forest and then cross the old Stone Bridge. Can you find your way by only moving in the direction of the arrows?

As Griselda crosses the bridge she meets a friendly wolf who tells her that the Centaur will guide her over the Blue Lake. Griselda rewards the wolf with a piece of cheese.

The Centaur helps Griselda through the Blue Lake and to the Old Witch's cottage.

start

end

The Old Witch and her friends discuss how to turn Rudy back into a frog. They must first solve the maze below.

Griselda is having a hard time remembering all of the witches' names. Can you figure out their names on the opposite page?

21

On her way home, Griselda runs into her friend Larry, who is a locksmith. Can you help them solve the key maze?

start

end

Griselda meets Carl on her way. His cart fell into a foxhole and broke its wheel. Griselda uses her magic to fix it. As a token of his appreciation, Carl gives Griselda a beautiful red cape. Can you figure out how the sly fox escaped to his den?

Griselda bumps into her friend Henry. He needs her help in getting to the other side of the lake. They can only move through the islands whose numbers add up to 13. Can you help Griselda and Henry solve the addition problems and cross the lake?

Griselda finally arrives home later that night. She is exhausted from a long day and falls immediately to sleep. While she sleeps, a hungry mouse tries to find its way to the cheese.

end

start

Griselda wakes up bright and early to get ready for the Witch Dance. Rudy is very excited too and begins to hop all around the room. Move through the frogs to see how Rudy can get from Start to End.

end

start

As the moon rises, Griselda makes her way to the Witch Dance in her new red cape. While she is flying, a group of bats get in her way; can you find a way out?

end

start

Griselda is almost there! The witches have started dancing. Help Griselda across the moon and then through the magic pentagon in order to meet up with them.

start

end

end

After the dance, the witches drink their special witch tea while the Forest Spirits put on a show. Can you find your way through the wacky Spirits?

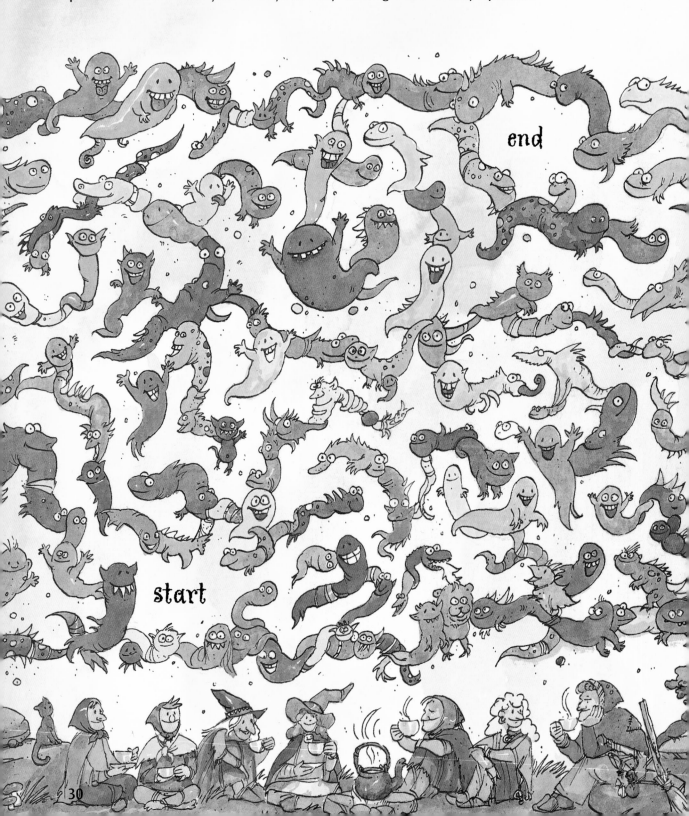

It's now time for the witches' pets to have a maze race.

Griselda leaves the party just before dawn.

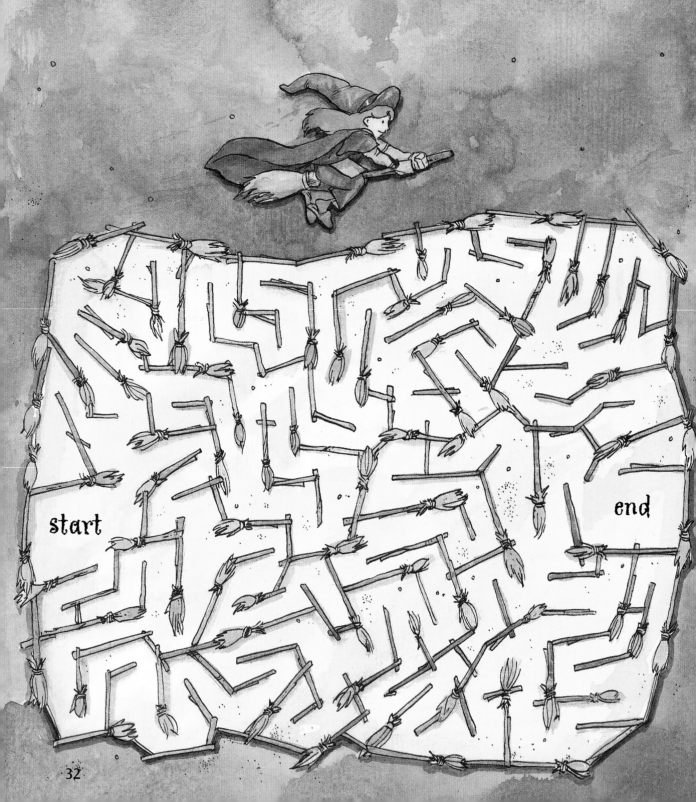

start

end

A couple of days later, Griselda invites all of her friends over for lunch.

start

end

Answers

page 6

page 7

page 8

page 9

pages 12–13

From
starting
point D

page 14

The owl brought the message to Griselda.

page 15

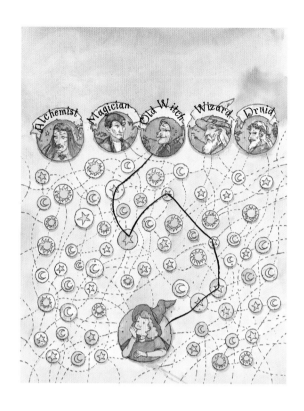

page 16

page 17

pages 20–21

A = Ingrid

B = Beatrice

C = Isabella

D = Heidi

E = Elise

page 22

page 23

page 24

page 25

38

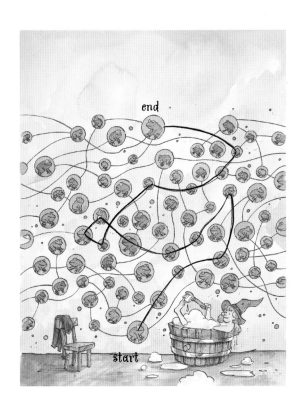

pages 28–29

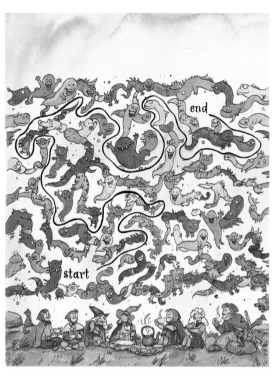